Things I Learned After It Was Too Late
(And Other Minor Truths)

Things I Learned After It Was Too Late
(And Other Minor Truths)

Charles M. Schulz

Holt, Rinehart and Winston **New York**

Published by Holt, Rinehart and Winston,
383 Madison Avenue, New York, New York 10017.

Published simultaneously in Canada by Holt, Rinehart
and Winston of Canada, Limited.

Printed in the United States of America

Things I Learned After It Was Too Late
(And Other Minor Truths)

He who lives by the dirty rotten little drop shot dies by the dirty rotten little drop shot!

**Nothing echoes
like an empty mailbox.**

**Unfortunately, it's very hard
to forget someone
by drinking root beer!**

Every time there's a good suggestion, someone brings up the budget!

**All the best coaches
are in the stands.**

**Subtraction is the awful feeling
that you know less today
than you did yesterday.**

My life is going by too fast....
My only hope is that
we go into overtime.

**There's a lot more to life
than not watching TV!**

The sins of the stomach are visited unto the body.

**To stay warm in winter,
insulate the ol' attic!**

When you have to get up at 7:00, 6:59 is the worst time of day!

**Joggers have to be careful—
it's easy to run
into a barbed comment!**

**Necks hate to exercise.
If necks were feet,
you'd never go anywhere.**

**When no one loves you,
you have to pretend
that everyone loves you.**

**Summers always fly...
winters walk!**

**When you're depressed,
it helps to lean your head on
your arm and stare into space—
if you're unusually depressed,
you may have to change arms.**

**No matter how hard you try,
you can't steer a dog dish!**

The worst thing about swimming is crossing a hot parking lot!

**If light travels so fast,
how come the afternoons
are so long?**

"How to grill a swordfish":
Ask him a lot of tough questions!

**A good education is
the next best thing
to a pushy mother!**

**Feet are always mad
about something....**

As soon as I get up in the morning, I feel like I'm in over my head.

If you hold your hands upside down, you get the opposite of what you pray for.

**The best trips are the kind
where you can be home by noon.**

**One of the great joys in life
is scarfing junk food!**

**If no one answers the phone,
dial louder.**

**You can't write a
term paper before breakfast.**

**Never drop a box of sequins
on a shag rug!**

Never lie in bed at night asking yourself questions you can't answer....

There's nothing more embarrassing than barking up the wrong tree!

There's a difference between a philosophy and a bumper sticker!

**Keep an eye on your lunch box
so it doesn't get ripped off.**

Life is easier if you only dread one day at a time.

Ten minutes before you go to a party is no time to be learning to dance!

**Never ask your secretary
to read something back**.

**Vitamin C does not keep
you from getting wet!**

Feet should stay awake in case you have to go some place in a hurry!

**Mention marriage to a musician,
and you get drowned out!**

**No matter how hard you try,
you can't build a rainman.**

**A watched supper dish
never fills.**

**Classes can ruin
your grade average!**

**No book on psychology
can be any good if
you can understand it!**

I'm always sure about things that are a matter of opinion.

**Lovers don't send
form letters.**

The late bird does not even catch the late worm!

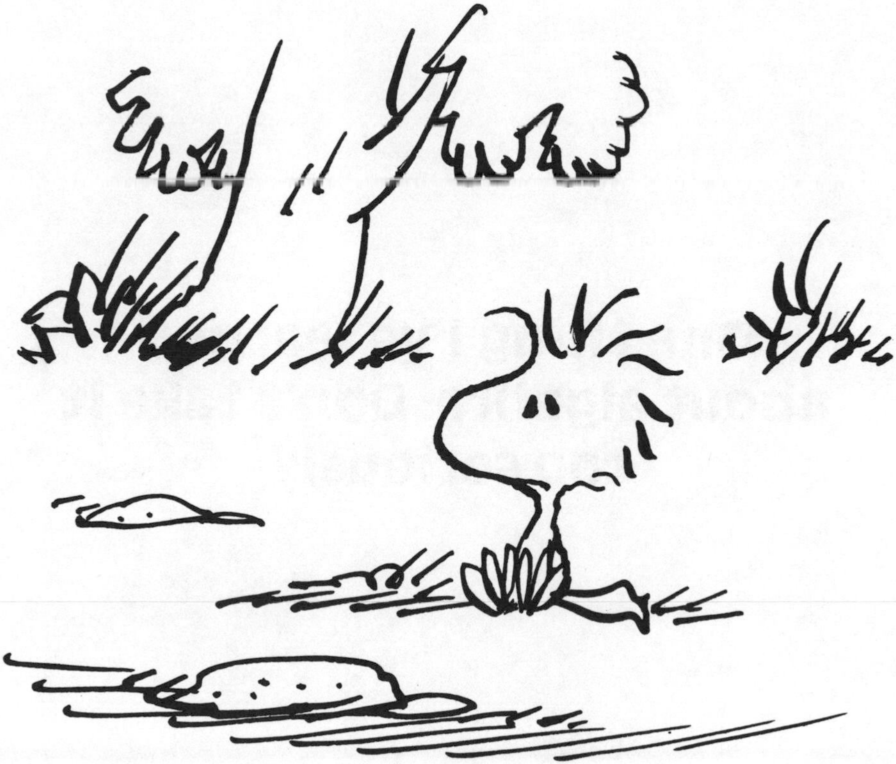

One thing I've learned about algebra: Don't take it too seriously.

**It's impossible to be gloomy
when you're sitting
behind a marshmallow.**

**Sidewalks always win...
knees always lose!**

**A thumb tastes best
at room temperature!**

**"Quiet beauty" is nice
to have, but it should
speak up now and then.**

**Never share your pad
with a restless bird!**

**Being crabby all day
makes you hungry.**

**When we lose, I'm miserable....
When we win, I feel guilty!**

**I would have won,
but I got off to a bad finish!**

**Life is like an ice cream cone:
You have to learn to lick it!**

**Don't blame people
who are born with crabby genes.**

**It's always difficult to talk
from one generation to another.**

**It's all right to look interested,
but looking bored
is easier on the eyes....**

**The secret to life is
to be in the right room!**

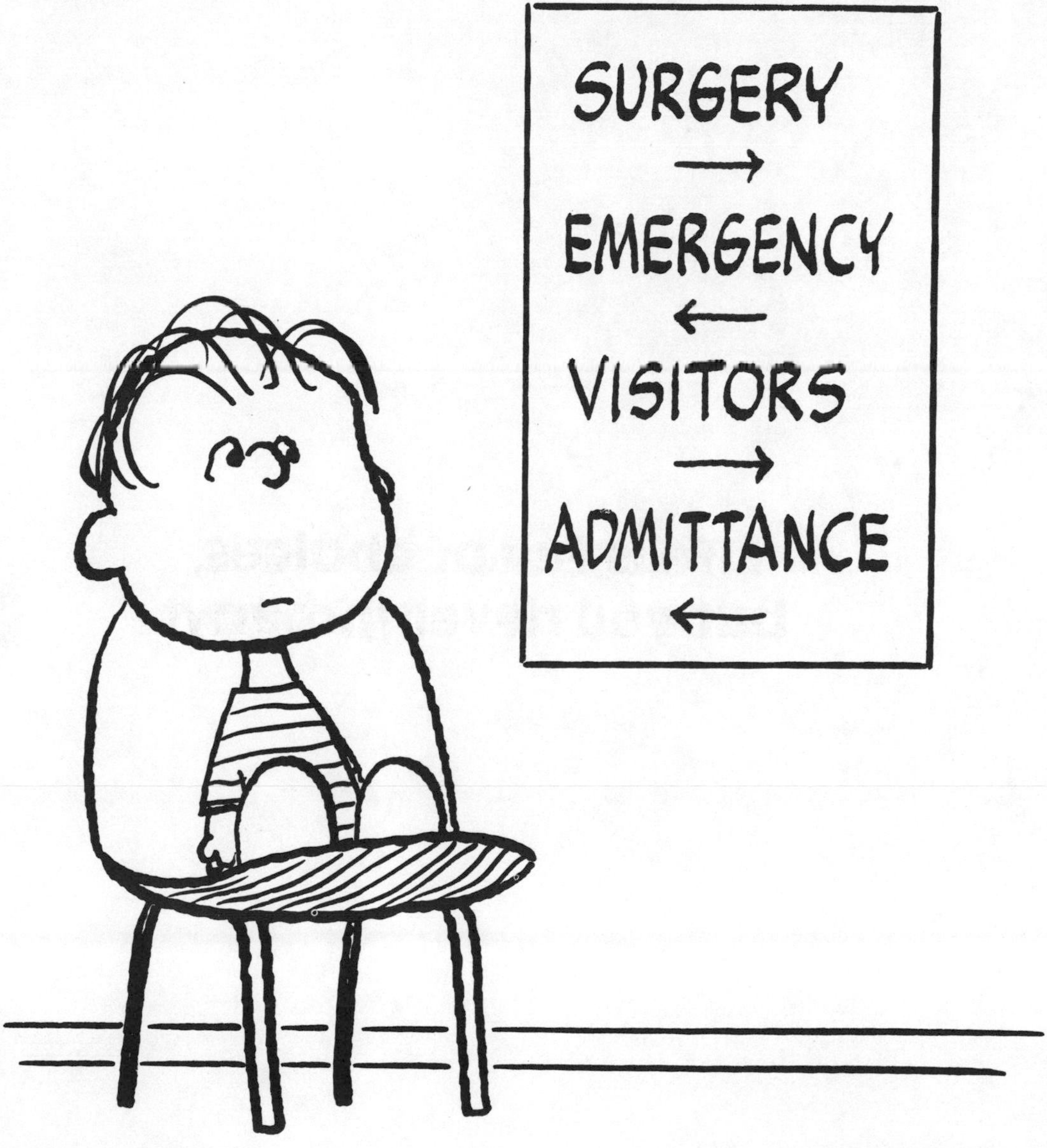
SURGERY →
EMERGENCY ←
VISITORS →
ADMITTANCE ←

**Life is full of choices,
but you never get any!**